I0140448

The Deepest Parts

Lander V. Stovall

STRIVE PUBLISHING
www.striveipg.com

Copyright © 2025 Lander V. Stovall

All Rights Reserved. No part of this publication may be reproduced, distributed, or transmitted in any form or by any means, including photocopying, recording, or other electronic or mechanical methods, without the prior written permission of the publisher, except in the case of brief quotations embodied in critical reviews and certain other noncommercial uses permitted by copyright law.

Strive International Publishing Group is a division of Courageous Media Group. For more information on the authors, ordering, book signings, or to sponsor an event, contact us at info@courageouswomanmag.com.

ISBN: 979-8-218-68301-6

Edited/formatted by Shonell Bacon
Publisher/Book Coach – Telishia Berry

Dedication

This book is dedicated to the woman I have become and to my daughter, Ni'Shawan; my granddaughters, Brandejah, Meagan, Morgan, Yasmine, and Ariyah; and those women who are still finding their way. I encourage you to never stop asking, seeking, and knocking. The doors are waiting to be opened, and no one will be able to shut them.

God has a special word for you.

> Whoever catches a glimpse of the revealed counsel of God – the free life! – even out of the corner of his eye, and sticks with it, is no distracted scatterbrain but a man or woman of action. That person will find delight and affirmation in the action. James 1:25, *The Message*

Acknowledgments

I want to acknowledge God the Father, the Son, and the Holy Spirit for allowing me to get to the other side of *Through*.

I would like to thank my children, Waymond and Ni'Shawn for their love, understanding and support during my times of testing and training.

Pastor Milton Coats, thank you for showing me the light at the end of the tunnel.

Special thanks to my Apostles, Ruthel and Scott Hinton, for recognizing and releasing me into my God-given purpose. I love you both.

And to my friend, Gloria Brandon, thank you for walking this walk of faith with me.

Table of Contents

August 26, 2010

Sometime during the joy of life, a whole person cracked.

She had been such a great thinker, a shaker and a mover. She was the one to get everybody motivated. If she said *push*, you had to push. She'd say you had to take one more step, one more breath. Just had to get it done. Whatever it took, get it done. Find your purpose and walk in it. God only made one like you, and only you qualify to be you. No one sees your vision like you. Like you, it is ever changing, ever evolving.

Despite her go-getter, encourager personality, each day, a little bit of her soul seeped out. While reflecting on how the fracture began, she had allowed other voices to speak into her heart, voices that were not the voice of God.

And ultimately, she lost her focus.

The amazing thing is God knew that she—and *you*, too—would finally reach the pinnacle, the top. Though diminishing self-confidence was ever-present, you continued to rise. You struggled until you decided to stop struggling. You gave it to the One who it truly belonged to in the first place. You always had the manual, but just like a parent putting a bike together on Christmas Eve, you tried to do it quick and without the manual. A lot of loose screws surrounded you on the floor upon your "completion," screws that God had to carefully put back in place.

But He couldn't just replace them one screw at a time.

No, He had to disassemble the whole thing, for He knew that it was perfect when He made it. And no matter how hard He tried, He had to break it, *you*, to fix it. But this time, He used *his* Super Glue. He poured the Holy Spirit inside the broken vessel and sealed it with the blood of Jesus, so no matter how hard you're knocked down, no matter how many times you fall, you would never be broken again.

He left you with the reassurance that no weapon formed against you shall prosper, that you are the head and not the tail, that greater is He that is in you than he that is in the world.

And should you feel a crack coming on, read the manual, read His word, read the Bible.

Jesus Standing on MY Feet

Jesus standing on my feet,
And I on his walking down the street,
Making sure I stay straight on the path
Until we meet.

Thank you, God, for my salvation
And helping me keep my sanctification.
You sent your Holy Spirit, and it's deep
down inside,
Sitting on my soul so I don't lose my stride.

With a three-fold cord, your Spirit ties my
will, emotion, and weakness,
As it releases your love, joy, and meekness.

I want to shout the "Good News" so
heaven can hear
Of your goodness, grace, and mercy,
But I hear that still small voice say, "I'm
always close. I'm always near.

"Just listen with your heart. As long as *you* want me, we will never part.
Remember, I knew you long before your start
As I was here before your beginning, and I will be here when you depart."

Lord, it is your face I seek. Sometimes, I can't hardly speak.
Will you give me a glimpse of heaven, just a little peek?
That's ok, I'll wait—it will be such a treat.

And you said, "I'll be at heaven's gate, just don't you be late."

Compromise

Compromise, compromise—wearing a disguise.

Compromise, compromise—leading to your demise.

Compromise, compromise—meeting your soul's desires.

Compromise, compromise—till your spirit man dies.

2004

New Year, New Year, 2004—said I would not do that no more.

Got my days mixed up, waited for you like the "night Before Christmas."

Only wanted one gift–LOVE–but I guess the North Pole is too cold.

Fell fast asleep, awaken to a hot cup of tea to hold.

Not so bad–tea is always there to soothe my soul.

The Fire

The fire of love — **Passion**

The fire of life — **Eternity**

The fire of light — **Learning**

Inspiration

Inspiration is the knock me down,

pick myself up,

go on about my business,

don't die yet,

finish what you started,

get it done,

keep on going,

that a girl,

move it, move it, move it,

mission accomplished,

Now I Can Breathe,

Aaaaaaaah.

Ice Cream

The loves of my life are in my past

Don't know why their love did not last

Like ice cream, they are gone too fast

Condition for the Condition

I loved you unconditionally.
There should be conditions for that condition.

I love you eternally.
Is there timeout in forever?
If there was, I forgot to take mine.

We have no control of who we love; it's a condition.
It's like parents—you have who you got.

The choices we make are in the present condition.
We know not the effect on the future condition,
For the choice was made from the past condition.
There must be a condition for that condition.

They Don't Know

People look at me and wonder
Why do I ponder the thought of you.

They don't know the man I know.
They don't know the man I see.
The man I see is all the man there could ever
be.

The man who painted my toes
And wiped my nose—the man who listened
to all my woes,
Washed my hair and dried it, too.
That man that's who.

They don't know the man that waited on me
hand and foot,
Kissed me from head to toe, holding me
tight, saying, I'll never let you go.
The one that got me hooked.
They don't know the man.

Defeated

Thank you for your part in my destruction.
Thank you for the lies,
The deceit—defeated.

I'll not try to help bring sunshine.
I'll not show love and be kind.

I'll not think of others anymore.
I'll think like others and even the score.

This world is so corrupt.
I'll join the world if I must.
I can't do that because in God I will trust.

I Wanna Know

I wanna know
Can I cry with you
Laugh with you

I wanna know
How long does the sweet talk last
Can we make love on the grass

I wanna know
In five years
Will you woo me still

I wanna know
Do you know hurt
Like I know hurt

I wanna know
Will you make my
Half-moon whole

I wanna know will you be my lover
My brother
My man
My yard man
My man's man

I wanna know—can you kiss me like that again
And again?

Leaving

Moving forward faster than a locomotive
out of control
God the Father, guide me to my heavenly
goal

Trying to do right
Cutting the ties that bind
Though it makes me feel so cold

Leaving the station—that station of sin
Trying not to lose my soul
Trying to take back what Satan stole

Feeling good from my head to my soles
From my nose to my fingertips.
Doing good everywhere I go
Telling all about God to everyone I meet

New York, New York

New York, New York
Hit hard by terrorists

Now young boys want to enlist
America now shakes its fist

Troop after troop
We start to deploy

These G.I. Joes are not toys
Army, Air Force, Navy, Marines, our boys

President takin bout starting the draft
All will soon know their craft

We don't know how long the terror will last
Soldiers so young they have no past, no past

Lord, I Think It's You!

It's New Year's Eve
One man calls, says he's going to leave

One man calls, says stay by the phone
All I get is a dial tone

One man calls, says I'll call when I get back
in the area
I know his wife is the barrier

Yes, Lord, I want my own man,
One that's tall, strong and can stand on his
own
I don't want one I have to fix up
I want one that I can look up to

Oh my Lord, I thinks it's you!!

I Prayed

I wrote nothing in 2002
I tried my best to do what
You wanted me to do

Though I stumbled and fell, I got up again
and again
I don't think I'm going to Hell

The last day, I found myself in church
In the Choir stand I did perch

I prayed for all I knew
I prayed they all knew you

I pray this year I'll do better
Follow your Word to the letter

I pray that you will help me keep it all
together

I Will Never Stop Trying

I never won a race,
But I never stop trying

I may never get where I'm going,
But I will never stop trying

I may never find true love,
But I will never stop trying

I may never…
But I will never stop trying

Is it Love or Lust?

Is it love or lust
That keeps us in touch?

Is it love or lust
That gives a human touch?

Is it love or lust
That makes us such and such?

Is it love or lust
That makes us not trust?

Is it love or lust
That make us hold our breath until we bust?

Is it love or lust
That make us pay so much, so much?

He loves me? He lust me not?
He lust me? He loves me not?
He loves me when he lusts me.
    He wins.
    I'm in sin.

Fifty Years Old

Fifty years old and I was never told
Life you repent for
Life does unfold
The world in 2003 about to explode

Fifty years old and I was never told
In 1963 you worried about equality
And the year 2000 you might never see
Nuclear weapons why won't they let them
be

Fifty years old and I was never told
Young men snatched from using condoms
To Operation Kuwait, Operation IRAQ
Freedom. Bombs not hearts going
BOOM* BOOM* BOOM

Fifty years old and I was never told
Wars would never end, we may never grow
old. NEVER TOLD *TOLD *TOLD

This Room

A love was born
    Died
        resurrected
In this room

In this room
    We made time
        Wasted time
        Spent time
In this room

In this room
    We laughed
    We cried
    We loved
In this room—in this room

It's Insane

Heart in hand to give to this man
Let him in my world
Let him in my land

Tried my dam-ne-dest to withstand
He is tall, Black, and tan

Moving now on foreign sand
Heart beating like a one-man band
Is this it, or am I totally insane

Before You

Nothing really mattered before you
I was living to die
Each day was a day closer to that final
journey
Before you

Now I want to take steps, not steps but run
back

Gather all the time I lost
Running for each day
Back into life, love, and living

Steps back to 42, steps back before I met you

A Tear for Me

When I awoke up this morning
And did not see
Your smile, your lips, your nose, nor your
eyes,
I cried for you. I missed your scent,
Then I shed a tear for me.
            And again?

I'm

I'm cool, I'm calm
I know how to get my freak on

I laugh, I cry
I look at the world today, and I sigh

I'm soulful, I'm spiritual
I can be downright lyrical

I'm young, I'm old
I have not always done as I was told

I'm good, I'm bad
I thank God for the lives I've had

I look, I see
I'm only good at being me

I Can Feel

I can feel the love oozing out of me

Slowly and deliberately being sucked out of me

But I don't see **MY** reflection in his eyes

I can feel my heart being torn apart

I did not see it from the start

As much as I know I still can't drive a stake in **his** heart

Just Git

Why should I cry
  On the inside

As I listen to your
  alibi

Go on tell me
  Goodbye

Don't try
    to slide

Just Git
    Sh*t

???WHY???

If we march to a different drum
Why did you join my parade?

Take Time

Everybody has a walk in the wilderness
Take time to get rid of the bitterness

Some habits you have to kick
'Cause if you don't, you will get sin sick

How Long

How
    Long
        Can
           You
               Ride
                  A
                    Mule
BEFORE HE
           Starts
               Acting
                  Like
                    An
                       ASS
                      ?

On MY Face

Down to the altar on my face

Asking God to come into this place, my space

Thanking my Savior for His words, stating his case

Knowing that I'm saved only by God's love and grace

Fighting Satan daily trying to win this race

God sent his Son to show me love

Jesus did His work then ascended like a dove

Holy Ghost keeps us till we reach heaven above

Why can't you see that's *sho-nuff* LOVE

About the Fall

A fall could be fast as lightening—ask Satan
A fall could be fast as lightening—stop hating
A fall could be fast—start planting
A fall could be fast when Satan goes hate planting

Grow

When will you spring up and grow
The more you know, the more you grow
Be a better person from head to toe
Grow

The Most High

I leave with a Bible
You leave with a beer
What is it about God do you really fear

When life gets tough
I run to my Father
You run to yours
The one who made all life rough

When I need you to cover
You go undercover
When I need the Holy Spirit to hover

I thought in God we would trust
Is it love or carnal lust

When you look at me, what do you see
It's not my anointing trying to flee

I fought long and hard to get here
Now I wonder is my God still near
It is God I want to obey,

But this flesh body made of clay
Sometimes causes my spirit to decay

I long to live in heaven on high,
But if I live this lie, I surely will die

On this earth, you can get high
But there is no high like being with the
Most High

I Am Female
Hear See Feel

I am female, hear me speak
I am female, hear me scream
I am female, hear me mourn
I am female, hear me sing

I am female, see my joy
I am female, see my heart
I am female, see my love

I am female, feel my soul
I am female, feel my spirit
I am female, feel my freedom
And again?

Song of Psalms (with a melody)

Lord, give me revelation power
As I seek your face today
Lord, give me peace and understanding
As I travel along the way
Lord, give me grace and mercy
And the words that I should say
For in your Shekinah Glory
It's where I want to stay

Psalms 91:1-3a
He that dwells in the secret place
Of the most High shall abide
Under the shadow to the Almighty
I will say of thee O Lord
For he is my refuge and my fortress
My God in him will I trust
Surely he will deliver me from the snare of
the fowler

Psalms 27:1-2
The Lord is light and my salvation
whom shall I fear

Lander V. Stovall

The Lord is the strength of my life
Of whom shall I be afraid
When the wicked even mine enemies
came upon me to eat up my flesh
they stumbled and fell

Psalms 1:1-2
Blessed is the that walked not
In the counsel of the ungodly
Not sitteth in the seat of the scornful
But his delight is in the law of the Lord
And in his law doth he meditate both day
night

Strong Woman Strong Woman

Strong Woman Strong Woman
You just keep on coming
Like a freight train pulling 30 cars
You keep your head lifted to the stars

Strong Woman Strong Woman
You just keep on coming some think you are extinct
But you just keep on using your instincts

Strong Woman Strong Woman
You treat your children real good
Like a real woman should
You are Proverbs 31, all your work is done

Strong Woman Strong Woman
Wish I could be you
I should have been you
But because of you I'm still here

Lander V. Stovall

Strong Woman Strong Woman
That's your name; you've got so much game
You can take a cracker and make it gourmet

Strong Woman Strong Woman
You roar like a lion
But can purr like a kitten
Especially when you have been smitten

Strong Woman Strong Woman
You love so hard, you love a lot
You love like the Lord
You give it all you got

Strong Woman Strong Woman
You stand so tall, you can stoop so low
But on your knees is when your prayers
flow

Strong Woman Strong Woman
So many good deeds
Because the Lord's voice you did heed
Now he provides all of your needs

Strong Woman Strong Woman
I look in your face when I feel disgrace
I move in your space
And like you strong woman
I wear lace

Remix of a Poem Lost in the Fire

Where are the Martin Luther Kings?
Riding in their limousines
Don't you want to hear the marchers sing?
WE shall overcome, let freedom ring
Where are the Martin Luther Kings?

Where are the Martin Luther Kings?
They used to be all in your neighborhoods
Now they all are up to no good
Wearing black hoods—can't blame the white hoods
Listen to the sirens just up to no good
Where are the Martin Luther Kings?

Where are the Martin Luther Kings?
We used to use our brains
Now they all locked up in chains
Some of them even gone insane
Where are the Martin Luther Kings?

Where are the Martin Luther Kings?
Riding in their limousines
Trying to sell that crack
Now we don't know how to act
We can get our freedom back
If we get on the knowledge track
Where are the Martin Luther Kings?

Where are the Martin Luther Kings?
Anything they throw at us we succeed
Threw the drugs in the hood
We came up now we can't breed
Threw the drugs in the hood
Killings Genocide they stole our seed
Where are the Martin Luther Kings?

Where are the Martin Luther Kings?
I miss those marchers sing
Wish those marchers could sing
Let freedom ring, we shall overcome
Now we are acting so dumb
Where are the Martin Luther Kings?

Where are the Martin Luther Kings?
Riding in their limousines
Got their nose in the air

Lander V. Stovall

Acting like they just don't care
Where are the Martin Luther Kings?

Where are the Martin Luther Kings?
He stood so tall with his back up against the
wall
He walked so far to get you up the hill
Now we are writing laws and signing bills
Where are the Martin Luther Kings?

Where are the Martin Luther Kings?
Come on Negros, African Americans, and
Black folk
We've come too far; it's not time to choke
We have a generation to help get a start
Before this world, all the marchers depart
Where are the Martin Luther Kings?

Where are the Martin Luther Kings?
We can look high and we can look low
WE have do more than let the lyrics flow
Use your talents, use your songs,
But most of all, we have got to stay strong
Where are the Martin Luther Kings?

I'm Just Your Water

You don't worry about water until you need
it.
When you turn it on, you want it to flow.
And when it flows, you need to know where
it will go.

Water will keep you afloat.
Water will float your boat.
Too much water will get your goat.

Water is what you drink.
It's not what you think.
Water supplies life and the afterlife.
Water sustains life, almost like a wife.

Some water you can't drink.
More water will make you sink.
Some water just stinks.

Water comes down slow, like the dew in the
morning
Comes and rests upon my heart.

Lander V. Stovall

Gently washes my face and creeps inside my space,
Rolls down my nose as a tear or washes the wax out of my ear.

Water wet—moves fast like white water current—like money… currency
swiftly or current see.

I'll be your bridge over troubled waters, or if you can't see, clear as water we'll just be water under the bridge.

Water is as subtle as a gentle stream, washing and rinsing in your midnight dreams.

Fast and furious as the great Niagara Fall but not as beautiful as you walking down the hall.

Water can be liquid, solid, or gas.
Love flows as liquid when it's sweet, goes above our heads as a gas, and when it's true, it is solid as a rock.

Water will drip drop drip until it enters a crack… then you slide in just like sin. If we marry, and we make that deal, keep it on lock like Thompson's water seal. And that's real.

So, when you find the man with the pitcher of water, follow him to the upper-room. You will find the man with living water, and there, you will find me hiding under the shadow of the wings of the almighty.

123, come and get me.

The Big Easy Is Un-Easy

January first, a murderous thirst brought
on a deadly curse.
It was around three when the spirits started
running free.
A man who had lost his mind but found
some energy.
He did the unthinkable on Bourbon Street.
Driving his truck through the barricades.
I think he came from Esplanade.

Wounded in his heart, but that's where it
starts
He picked up some of the pieces, but they
are all not there.
You could see his hopeless stare and smell
the danger in the air.

As Jon Batiste and Lil Weezy exclaimed,
"The city feels uneasy."
The people were out celebrating.
Dressed in few clothes, a little sleezy,
always feeling breezy.

Anything goes, as you take that stroll,
further down Bourbon Street.
Women dancing on poles. They climb
down, hearing the sirens wail.
Acting like they just don't care.
A familiar sound, someone caught in a
snare.
Breathing heavy like a hard-working mare.

Taking everything to the limits. Most of
their hearts are not in it.
Let me do it one last time.
Let me bring in the New Year on someone
else's dime.
They never went there looking for fear.
Now fifteen people are dead as the city
sheds a tear.

The city feels uneasy.
Locked down on January one. Everything
that was planned was dead before the
rising of the sun.
The Big Easy can't stay uneasy. They have
to continue to move on for those who came
for the Super Bowl game.

Lander V. Stovall

Rest assured like the Mighty Mississippi,
the Big Easy will still roll on.
Another "Second Line" sure as you're born.

America, We Have to Do Better!
Back the Blue

Alton Sterling Protests

America the red, white, and blue
That includes me, and that includes you
Right now, it seems we are black and blue
Not talking about color or uniform
Talking about the situation.
We are hurting, and it shows

America is black and blue
When the country has been hit
The blood runs hot, the blood rushes to the
surface of our skin,
We are all human, we are all kin

America is black and blue
It leaves a scar when one of us is shot dead
in a car
It leaves a scar when one of us is shot on the
ground

Lander V. Stovall

It seems like no love can be found, but,
America, love must abound
This makes no sense, cops killed in the line
duty, under fire with no defense

America is black and blue
Float like a butterfly, sting like a bee,
We all want to be free
Float like a butterfly, sting like a bee
America, open your eyes, can't you see, we
are the greatest, just like Ali

America is black and blue
Upper cut, Black man dead, right cross,
Black man dead.
One two, right jab, officers down in Dallas,
left cross, officers dead in Baton Rouge
We all want those days back if we could. We
all, to see our loved ones alive, yes we would

We have lost the fight, but if we move
toward the light the battle is not over.
We have to take action. Love is the answer;
we can't just wish on a four-leaf clover
Just look deep inside and know, America,
we are better than this

Have you ever slapped yourself in the face?
That's America when we divide ourselves
by our race
America is red, white, yellow, black, and
blue. We have to get it together; this, we
must do.

America is black and blue.
It takes time to heal, the sooner the better we
will feel.

www.ingramcontent.com/pod-product-compliance
Lightning Source LLC
Chambersburg PA
CBHW070027110426
42741CB00034B/2672